Editor
Eric Migliaccio

Managing Editor
Ina Massler Levin, M.A.

Cover Artist
Barb Lorseyedi

Illustrator
Sue Fullam

Art Production Manager
Kevin Barnes

Imaging
Rosa C. See

Publisher
Mary D. Smith, M.S. Ed.

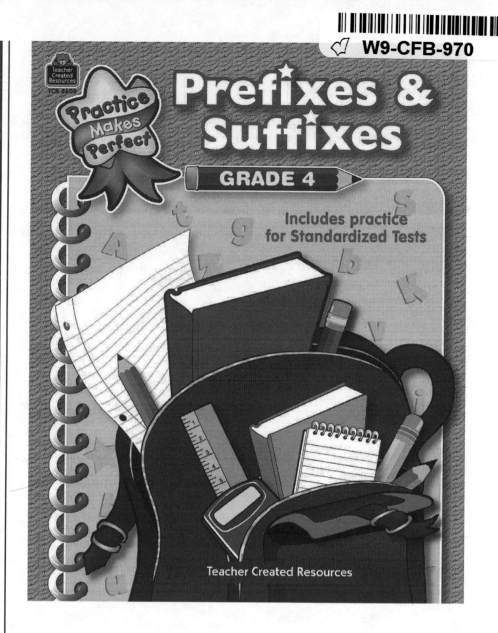

Practice Makes Perfect
Prefixes & Suffixes
GRADE 4

Includes practice for Standardized Tests

Teacher Created Resources

Author

Debra J. Housel, M.S. Ed.

Teacher Created Resources

Teacher Created Resources, Inc.
6421 Industry Way
Westminster, CA 92683
www.teachercreated.com

ISBN: 978-1-4206-8608-1

©2006 Teacher Created Resources, Inc.
Reprinted, 2015
Made in U.S.A.

Table of Contents

Introduction

The old adage "practice makes perfect" can apply to your child and his or her education. The more practice and exposure your child has with concepts being taught in school, the more success he or she is likely to find. For many parents, knowing how to help their children may be frustrating because the resources may not be readily available. As a parent, it is also hard to know where to focus your efforts so that the extra practice your child receives at home supports what he or she is learning in school.

A child's ability to comprehend what he or she reads depends upon the ability to understand the meaning of new words when they are encountered. A knowledge of prefixes and suffixes helps your student to quickly grasp the meaning of unknown words. This knowledge also serves an important role in expanding a student's vocabulary and spelling abilities. *Practice Makes Perfect: Prefixes and Suffixes, Grade 4* covers the prefixes and suffixes most frequently used in words found in both fiction and nonfiction text. A chart on page 45 shows the meanings of all of the prefixes and suffixes covered.

The exercises included in this book meet or reinforce educational standards and objectives similar to the ones required by your state and school district for fourth-graders:

- The student will recognize and know the meaning of common prefixes and suffixes.

- The student will use a knowledge of prefixes and suffixes to decode unknown words.

- The student will use a knowledge of prefixes and suffixes to determine the meaning of new words.

- The student will use a knowledge of prefixes and suffixes in order to spell words correctly.

How to Make the Most of This Book

Here are some ideas for making the best use of this book:

- Set aside a specific place in your home to work on this book. Keep the necessary materials on hand.

- Determine a specific time of day to work on these practice pages to establish consistency. Look for times in your day or week that are conducive to practicing skills.

- Keep all practice sessions with your child positive and constructive. If your child becomes frustrated or tense, set aside the book and look for another time to practice.

- Allow the child to use whatever writing instrument he or she prefers.

- Review and praise the work your child has done.

- Assist the student in understanding directions and decoding sentences.

- Promote good test-taking skills on every page by telling your child, "Do the ones you know first. Then go back and figure out the rest."

- Encourage the child to point out words with prefixes or suffixes in the materials he or she reads.

The Prefix *mis-*

The prefix *mis-* means "wrong."

Thinking of the word *mistake* will help you to remember the meaning.

   Example: *misuse* means "wrong use"

Part I: Add the prefix *mis* to the base word to form a new word.

   Example: pronounce   **mispronounce**

1. print _____

2. fit _____

3. spoke _____

4. judge _____

5. spell _____

6. placed _____

7. fire _____

8. leading _____

9. match _____

10. informed _____

11. treat _____

12. fortune _____

Part II: Write a word from the box below that means the opposite of the word or phrase given.

misfortune	mistake	mismanaged	misbehavior
mismatched	mislabel	mislead	misspelled
misjudge	misprint	misquote	~~misunderstood~~

Word	Opposite	Word	Opposite
1. understood	misunderstood	7. label correctly	_____
2. matched	_____	8. quote exactly	_____
3. good behavior	_____	9. print correctly	_____
4. good fortune	_____	10. correct	_____
5. spelled right	_____	11. lead correctly	_____
6. well managed	_____	12. judge correctly	_____

More Practice with the Prefix *mis-*

The prefix *mis-* means "wrong."

misshapen	misbehaved	misleading	mismatched	misprinted	misspelled
misfortune	mistake	misplaced	misquoted	mismanaged	misunderstanding

Part I: Choose the word from the box above that best completes each sentence and write it on the line. Each word is used once.

1. I had a perfect grade because I didn't make a single _____ on the test.

2. Emma thought it was great fun to wear _____ shoes, one green and one red.

3. The company was so _____ that it lost money for six years in a row.

4. The time on the invitations was _____ , so they had to be reprinted.

5. The customers were angry because the ad was so _____ .

6. Grandma has _____ her eyeglasses again.

7. The newspaper _____ Mrs. Georger; that's not what she actually said.

8. The trucker had the _____ of getting stuck in a three-hour traffic jam.

9. The child only _____ because she was so hot and tired.

10. Ever since their _____ , they haven't spoken to each other.

11. The heat had melted the chocolate bar into a _____ lump.

12. Colby lost the spelling bee when he _____ the word *judgmental*.

Part II: Pick two words from the box above. Use each in a sentence.

Example: ___He had a **misunderstanding** with his best friend.___

1. _____

_____

2. _____

_____

The Prefix over-

The prefix *over-* means "over (across or above)" or "too much."

Examples: *overpass* means "over (above) the highway"

overpaid means "paid too much"

Part I: Add the prefix *over* to the words below to form a word that fits the definition given. Write the word on the line.

board	lap	~~heard~~	looked	slept	eat
grown	weight	cooked	time	due	seas

1. he heard what he shouldn't have heard   overheard

2. roast cooked too much   _____

3. grass grown too much   _____

4. didn't notice; looked without seeing   _____

5. eat too much   _____

6. fall off of a ship   _____

7. past the time it was to be turned in   _____

8. go across the ocean   _____

9. pieces that cross over each other   _____

10. weigh too much   _____

11. work longer than normal hours   _____

12. slept too much   _____

Part II: Write a word beginning with the prefix *over* that means the opposite of the **boldface** phrase. Use words from the 12 words above.

Example: He worked a **short time**.   He worked   overtime

1. The teen was **too thin**.   The teen was _____.

2. The papers' edges **don't meet**.   The papers' edges _____.

3. She **noticed** every detail.   She _____ every detail.

4. Hayley **woke up on time**.   Hayley _____.

5. The book was **returned on time**.   The book was _____.

6. The bushes were **trimmed**.   The bushes were _____.

More Practice with the Prefix *over-*

The prefix *over-* means "over (across or above)" or "too much."

overboard	overgrown	overdue	overflowed	overwhelmed	overlap
overpass	overcooked	overweight	overseas	overlooked	overslept

Part I: Choose the word from the box above that best completes each sentence and write it on the line. Each word is used once.

1. The little child felt _____ by the loud noises.

2. When she forgot to shut off the faucet, the sink _____.

3. Jacob _____, which made him late getting to school.

4. The doctor put the _____ man on a diet.

5. Be sure to _____ the edges and press them down with glue.

6. The highway _____ bridge iced up before the road did.

7. My cousin, who is in the Navy, is serving _____ for two years.

8. It is dangerous to fall _____ on a ship.

9. The castle stood on a cliff that _____ the sea.

10. The thicket was so _____ that we couldn't move through it.

11. The _____ meat was too dry.

12. Bryan returned the three _____ DVDs to the library.

Part II: Pick two words from the box above. Use each in a sentence.

Example: __If you eat a lot of candy, you may become **overweight.**__

1. _____

_____

2. _____

_____

The Prefix *co-*

The prefix *co-* means "together."

Examples: *copilot* means "pilot together" (there are at least two navigators)

cooperate means "operate together" (work together)

Part I: Match the word to its meaning. Write the letter on the line next to the word.

_____ 1. coincidence

a. person who owns something together with another person

_____ 2. cosign

b. exist together in the same time or place

_____ 3. co-starring

c. person who brings together (coordinates things)

_____ 4. co-pay

d. authored (written) together

_____ 5. coexist

e. sign together

_____ 6. cooperate

f. things that occur together; happen at the same time

_____ 7. co-author

g. operate together; work together

_____ 8. copilot

h. starring together (like actors in a movie)

_____ 9. co-owner

i. pilot together

_____ 10. coordinator

j. pay together; shared payment

Part II: Put a ✓ next to those words that could mean a person.

co-star	_____	cosign	_____	coincidence	_____
copilot	_____	co-host	_____	co-payment	_____
coexist	_____	co-owner	_____	coworker	_____
coordinator	_____	co-author	_____	cooperate	_____

copilot

copilot

copilot

copilot

More Practice with the Prefix *co-*

The prefix *co-* means "together."

co-author	copilot	coworker	cosign	co-star	co-payment
co-hosts	cooperate	coincidence	coordinator	coexist	co-owners

Part I: Choose from the box above the word that best completes each sentence and write it on the line. Each word is used once.

1. Did you intend to meet me here, or was it just a _____?

2. The tutoring _____ arranged for Shelby to have a tutor for math.

3. As she left the cockpit, the pilot asked her _____ to take over the controls.

4. Since both of their names on are on the house deed, they must be _____.

5. My insurance plan requires a $20 _____ for every visit to the doctor.

6. If you'll just _____, we'll get done much faster.

7. He and his _____ will autograph their books at the bookstore next Monday.

8. Since Cody is just 17, his mom had to_____ on his car loan.

9. Some television talk shows have several _____.

10. The man asked a _____ to help him write the report.

11. Cactus and seaweed cannot _____ because they need different environments.

12. Brad Pitt and Kate Winslett _____ in that new movie.

Part II: Pick two words from the box above. Use each in a sentence.

Example: The party **coordinator** made all the arrangements for my birthday party.

1. _____

_____

2. _____

_____

The Prefix *multi-*

The prefix *multi-* means "many."

> *Examples:* *multicultural* means "involving many cultures"
>
> *multilingual* means "knowing many languages"

Part I: Form words by adding *multi* to the base word. Write the word on the line.

Example: national __multinational__

1. media _____

2. level _____

3. colored _____

4. tasking _____

5. family _____

6. purpose _____

7. millionaire _____

8. lingual _____

Part II: Match the word to its meaning. Write the letter on the line next to the word.

_____ 1. multitasking

_____ 2. multiplication

_____ 3. multinational

_____ 4. multicolored

_____ 5. multifamily

_____ 6. multimillionaire

_____ 7. multilevel

_____ 8. multimedia

_____ 9. multiple

_____ 10. multitude

_____ 11. multipurpose

_____ 12. multilingual

a. a person who has several million dollars

b. having many levels (as in an office or apartment building)

c. using more than one media (words, pictures, and sound)

d. doing several tasks (jobs) at the same time

e. having more than one use, or purpose

f. a large group or crowd

g. a fast way to "add" the same number many times

h. knowing many languages

i. involving many nations

j. having many of something (such as children or injuries)

k. involving many families

l. having many colors

More Practice with the Prefix *multi-*

The prefix *multi-* means "many."

multitude	multitasking	multicolored	multilevel	multimillionaire	multicultural
multiple	multimedia	multipurpose	multifamily	multilingual	multiplication

Part I: Choose from the box above the word that best completes each sentence and write it on the line. Each word is used once.

1. Baking soda is a _____ item used to bake, to clean, and to deodorize.

2. The _____ event honored people with different customs and traditions.

3. Together, the Jansens, Dankens, and Grivolvos held a _____ yard sale.

4. If you get the _____ top, you can wear it with lots of different things.

5. Ami found it easy to remember _____ and division facts.

6. I was glad to see that it was a _____ choice test.

7. A stadium has _____ seating to give the audience the best view.

8. Often a professional athlete becomes a _____ due to a high income.

9. Since she can read, write, and speak four languages, Morgan is _____.

10. Mr. Edwards showed his _____ presentation to the board of directors.

11. Emilia had a _____ of questions for the guest speaker.

12. If you watch TV while washing dishes and talking on the phone, you are _____.

Part II: Pick two words from the box above. Use each in a sentence.

Example: I think double-digit **multiplication** is challenging.

1. _____

_____

2. _____

_____

The Prefixes *auto-* and *self-*

The prefix *auto-* means "self."

The prefix *self-* means "self" and is followed by a hyphen.

Examples: automobile means "move by itself" (car)

automatic means "operate by itself"

self-employed means "employed by one's own self"

Part I: Match the word to its meaning. Write the letter on the line next to the word

_____ 1. autonomy		a.	pilot (operate) by itself
_____ 2. automatic		b.	life story written by own self
_____ 3. autopilot		c.	self-government
_____ 4. autograph		d.	something that moves itself (car, vehicle)
_____ 5. automobile		e.	receiving banking services by oneself
_____ 6. autobiography		f.	operating by itself
_____ 7. automated teller machine (ATM)		g.	signature (writing) of oneself

Part II: Add the prefix *self-* to each of the following words to form a new word.

Example: insured ___self-insured___

1. confident	_____	6. centered	_____
2. help	_____	7. respect	_____
3. interest	_____	8. defense	_____
4. employed	_____	9. taught	_____
5. destruct	_____	10. pity	_____

More Practice with the Prefixes *auto-* and *self-*

The prefix *auto-* means "self." The prefix *self-* means "self" and is followed by a hyphen.

automobile	autograph	self-destruct	automatic	self-defense	self-employed
self-taught	automated	self-control	autopilot	self-pity	self-confident

Part I: Choose the word from the box above that best completes each sentence and write it on the line. Each word is used once.

1. The _____ girl stepped onto the stage and started to sing.

2. For safety's sake, the women took a class in _____.

3. The _____ mechanic repaired the car.

4. A bomb will always _____ when it explodes.

5. The famous tennis player wrote her _____ on my magazine cover.

6. He never took classes in piano; he is a _____ pianist.

7. While an airliner is in flight, the pilots sometimes turn on the _____.

8. If you wallow in _____, you won't get any better or make any progress.

9. By using _____, you can keep focused, even in a bad or scary situation.

10. When a doctor taps your knee, your body's _____ response is to move the knee.

11. When assembly lines become _____, people may lose their jobs.

12. My mom is _____; she owns her own business.

Part II: Pick two words from the box above. Use each in a sentence.

Example: I am a **self-taught** snowboard rider.

1. _____

_____

2. _____

_____

The Prefixes *in-* and *il-*

The prefixes *in-* and *il-* mean "not." The prefix *il-* is added to base words that begin with the letter *l*. The prefix *in-* is added to most other words.

> Examples: *incapable* means "not capable"
>
> *illegible* means "not legible" (not able to be read)

Part I: Write the meaning for each word.

Example: inseparable _____ not able to be separated _____

1. incorrect _____
2. illogical _____
3. informal _____
4. independent _____
5. invisible _____

6. illegal _____
7. insane _____
8. inaccurate _____
9. incomplete _____
10. ineffective _____

An *antonym* is a word that means the opposite of another. *Sincere* and *insincere* are antonyms.

Part II: Add the prefix *in-* or *il-* to change each word to its antonym.

Example: ability _____ inability _____

1. secure _____
2. action _____
3. legal _____
4. expensive _____
5. logical _____

6. frequent _____
7. legible _____
8. direct _____
9. justice _____
10. literate (able to read/write) _____

This is very hard to read.

illegible

illegible

illegible

illegible

More Practice with the Prefixes *in-* and *il-*

The prefixes *in-* and *il-* mean "not."

incapable	inaccurate	independent	illiterate	invisible	ineffective
illegal	infrequently	incorrect	illegible	illogical	informal

Part I: Choose from the box above the word that best completes each sentence and write it on the line. Each word is used once.

1. The new law made texting while driving _____ in our state.

2. Tom's arrow missed the target because his aim was _____.

3. That medicine was _____ for curing the flu.

4. Tuxedos won't be needed because the event is _____.

5. It's _____ to forecast a snowstorm when the air temperature is 100°F.

6. It's quiet here because trains _____ travel on these tracks.

7. The teacher marked six wrong answers _____.

8. A doctor's signature is often so hard to read that it's completely _____.

9. This is an _____ project that you cannot do with your classmates.

10. Since it's in this room but I can't see it, it must be _____.

11. A newborn human baby is _____ of walking right away.

12. You are literate because you can read and write, but a toddler is _____.

Part II: Pick two words from the box above. Use each in a sentence.

Example: I am **incapable** of being in two places at the same time.

1. _____

_____

2. _____

_____

The Prefixes *cent-* and *semi-*

The prefix *cent-* means "100."

The prefix *semi-* means "half."

Examples: *centennial* means "100th anniversary"

percent* means "per 100" (out of 100)

semisolid means "half solid"

* The *cent* comes at the end because it was originally two separate words: per cent.

Do the math problems. Match the numbers to find the answers. Write the word on the line.

cents (48)	century (16)	centennial (27)	percent (7)
centimeter (12)	centipede (6)	semicircle (5)	semester (21)
semicolon (3)	semifinal (8)	semiretired (9)	semiannual (35)

Example: There are 100 of these in $1 (6 x 8) _____ cents (6 x 8 = 48) _____

1. Another word for a half circle is (30 ÷ 6) _____

2. The name for a 100th anniversary (3 x 9) _____

3. A number compared to 100 (28 ÷ 4) _____

4. One-hundredth of a meter (2 x 6) _____

5. Half of a school year (3 x 7) _____

6. Still working part-time (72 ÷ 8) _____

7. A quarter is worth 25 (8 x 6) _____

8. One hundred years (4 x 4) _____

9. A contest before the final contest (56 ÷ 7) _____

10. Happening every half year (5 x 7) _____

11. A type of bug with many legs* (54 ÷ 9) _____

12. Punctuation mark that joins two complete sentences (18 ÷ 6) _____

* Incorrectly named because people thought that it had 100 feet; it doesn't.

More Practice with the Prefixes *cent-* and *semi-*

The prefix *cent-* means "100." The prefix *semi-* means "half."

century	centennial	semisolid	semifinals	centimeters	semicolon
semicircle	semiretired	percent	semester	centipede	cents

Part I: Choose from the box above the word that best completes each sentence and write it on the line. Each word is used once.

1. At the turn of the 20th _____ , computers hadn't been invented yet.

2. The _____ judge went to court only twice a week.

3. Fifty _____ is the same as one-half.

4. Mrs. Elbason gave me 75 _____ for sweeping her sidewalk.

5. Pudding is an example of a _____.

6. This _____ I plan to earn straight A's in all my subjects.

7. We arranged the desks in a _____ around the screen.

8. The _____ crawled slowly across the fallen log.

9. A _____ can be used to join two related sentences.

10. The town celebrated its _____ with a fireworks display.

11. Eric failed to qualify in the _____, so he won't be going to the finals.

12. The measurement was given in _____.

Part II: Pick two words from the box above. Use each in a sentence.

Example: ___I am going to a new school next **semester** .___

1. _____

_____

2. _____

_____

The Suffix *-tion*

The suffix *-tion* means "state or quality of." It is pronounced "shun." Adding the suffix *-tion* usually changes a word into a noun (thing).

> *Examples:* *fascination* means "state of being fascinated"
> *option* means "having the quality of opting" (choosing)

Part I: Change these words into nouns by adding *-tion* as a suffix. Check the spelling of the starred words in the dictionary before writing them on the lines.

Example: move* _____motion_____

1. attend* _____

2. invent _____

3. pollute* _____

4. direct _____

5. revolve* _____

6. reflect _____

7. explain* _____

8. complete* _____

9. determine* _____

10. protect _____

11. react _____

12. quote* _____

13. repeat* _____

14. prevent _____

15. combine* _____

16. exclaim* _____

* The spelling of a base word that ends in a letter other than *t* always changes when the suffix *-tion* is added.

Part II: Look at the changes you made to the starred words above. Write the words on the correct stars below.

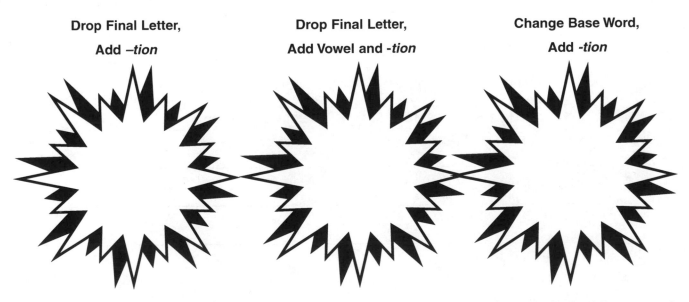

Drop Final Letter, Add *-tion*

Drop Final Letter, Add Vowel and *-tion*

Change Base Word, Add *-tion*

More Practice with the Suffix *-tion*

The suffix *-tion* means "state or quality of."

attention	caution	pollution	invention	motion	direction
quotation	suggestion	options	repetition	reflection	location

Part I: Choose from the box above the word that best completes each sentence and write it on the line. Each word is used once.

1. The key to learning math facts is _____.

2. To show when someone is speaking, enclose words inside _____ marks.

3. The _____ of the train lulled the child to sleep.

4. Jeremy couldn't pay _____ due to the noise and activity that surrounded him.

5. The SWAT team used _____ as it moved in closer.

6. In what _____ is that bus heading?

7. The factory's waste caused _____ that made the river's water unsafe.

8. May I make a _____?

9. Her latest _____ prevents snow from sticking to roads.

10. Nestled on the lake's shore, the _____ of their summer cottage was ideal.

11. It wasn't easy to make a choice because there were so many _____.

12. The puppy barked at its own _____ in the mirror.

Part II: Pick two words from the box above. Use each in a sentence.

Example: ___I wanted to hear all the **options** before I made a choice.___

1. _____

_____

2. _____

_____

The Suffix *-sion*

The prefix *-sion* means "state or quality of." It is pronounced "shun." When *-sion* is added to a verb (action word), it changes the word to a noun.

Examples: collision is what occurs when things collide (come into contact with each other)

decision is the result of a person deciding (making a choice)

Part I: Add *-sion* to each of the following verbs to form a noun. Check the spelling of the starred words in the dictionary before writing them on the lines.

Example: expand* _____expansion_____

1. confess _____
2. include* _____
3. televise* _____
4. discuss _____
5. admit* _____

6. comprehend* _____
7. profess _____
8. extend* _____
9. invade* _____
10. conclude* _____

* The spelling of a verb that ends in a letter other than *s* always changes when the suffix *-sion* is added.

Part II: Name the verb that is the basis for each of the following nouns. If you get stumped, you may use a dictionary.

Example: erosion _____erode_____

1. decision _____
2. division _____
3. exclusion _____
4. conclusion _____
5. explosion _____

6. revision _____
7. invasion _____
8. tension _____
9. confusion _____
10. permission _____

explosion

explosion

explosion

explosion

More Practice with the Suffix *-sion*

The prefix *-sion* means "state or quality of."

confusion	decision	collision	division	revision	discussion
television	professions	permission	explosion	admission	conclusion

Part I: Choose from the box above the word that best completes each sentence and write it on the line. Each word is used once.

1. What _____ can you draw from these clues?

2. Some parents limit the number of hours of _____ their kids may watch.

3. Most written work goes through at least one _____.

4. The opposite operation to multiplication is _____.

5. In all the _____, Matt got separated from his sister.

6. Today many _____ require a worker to have a college degree.

7. The _____ to the musical is $8.

8. His mother gave him _____ to sleep over at his friend's house.

9. The icy roads caused the _____.

10. We held a class _____ about how to solve the problem.

11. The bomb's _____ was so loud that people heard it three miles away.

12. Stacy made the _____ to study every single day.

Part II: Pick two words from the box above. Use each in a sentence.

Example: _The **collision** wrecked the car._

1. _____

_____

2. _____

_____

The Suffix *-ist*

The suffix *-ist* is "a person who does or a person who practices."

> *Examples:* a *florist* is a person who works with flowers
>
> a *pharmacist* is a person who works in a pharmacy (preparing and selling medicines)

Part I: Write the meaning of each of the words below.

Example: optimist _____person who practices optimism_____

1. artist _____

2. bicyclist _____

3. colonist _____

4. pianist _____

5. terrorist _____

6. stylist _____

7. biologist _____

8. tourist _____

9. dentist _____

10. typist _____

Part II: Change each word into an occupation that ends in the suffix *-ist*.

Example: bicycle* _____bicyclist_____

1. special _____

2. science* _____

3. solo _____

4. pharmacy* _____

5. journal _____

6. chemistry* _____

7. piano* _____

8. type* _____

9. motor _____

10. organ _____

* You will have to change the spelling of the base word before you add the suffix *-ist*.

chemist

chemist

chemist

chemist

More Practice with the Suffix *-ist*

The suffix *-ist* is "a person who does or a person who practices."

dentist	pharmacist	florist	scientist	chemist	colonist
artist	optimist	tourist	cyclist	pianist	journalist

Part I: Choose from the box above the word that best completes each sentence and write it on the line. Each word is used once.

1. A _____ often works in one field (area) of science.

2. Myla always sees the bright side of things because she's an _____.

3. The _____ was proud to have his sculpture displayed in an art gallery.

4. The Grand Canyon is a popular _____ attraction in Arizona.

5. Fortunately, the _____ wasn't injured when a car hit her bike.

6. The job of a _____ is to arrange flowers in a vase, bowl, or basket.

7. She got a job as a _____ at a well-known newspaper.

8. The _____ played a difficult piece by Bach.

9. A _____ recorded the details of the first Thanksgiving in her diary.

10. A _____ does experiments with chemicals.

11. The _____ filled a cavity in the girl's tooth.

12. Our _____ can fill the prescription within half an hour.

Part II: Pick two words from the box above. Use each in a sentence.

Example: __The teacher said that my friend may grow up to be an **artist**.__

1. _____

_____

2. _____

_____

The Suffix *-ic*

The suffix *-ic* means "related to." Adding *-ic* to a word usually makes it an adjective (describing word).

    Examples: *medic* means "related to medicine" (person who provides emergency medical aid)

                    comic means "related to comedy"

Part I: Add the suffix *-ic* to the base words to form adjectives. Refer to a dictionary to find the correct spelling of the starred words before writing them on the lines.

    Example: tragedy*   tragic

1. realist _____
2. volcano* _____
3. romance* _____
4. angel _____
5. drama* _____
6. period _____

7. hero _____
8. gymnast _____
9. science* _____
10. scene* _____
11. robot _____
12. history* _____

    * This base word changes when the suffix *-ic* is added.

Part II: Write the meaning of these words.

    Example: periodic   related to a period of time

1. electric _____
2. allergic _____
3. robotic _____
4. gigantic _____
5. horrific _____

6. strategic _____
7. economic _____
8. tragic _____
9. volcanic _____
10. metallic _____

volcanic

volcanic

volcanic

volcanic

More Practice with the Suffix *-ic*

The suffix *-ic* means "related to."

historic	tragic	medic	scenic	allergic	realistic
volcanic	comic	metallic	gigantic	electric	gymnastic

Part I: Choose from the box above the word that best completes each sentence and write it on the line. Each word is used once.

1. The _____ sign was so big that it was unstable, and the wind blew it over.

2. Thomas Edison invented the _____ light bulb.

3. I can't own a collie because I'm _____ to dog hair.

4. The loss of life caused by the flood was _____.

5. The _____ in the ambulance did CPR on the man.

6. It's not _____ to think that you can get all that done in one hour.

7. Whatever was in the box made a _____ sound when shaken.

8. The Declaration of Independence is a _____ document.

9. Since Damian liked superheroes, Cory got a new _____ book for him to read.

10. This road is called a _____ drive because it has so many pretty sights.

11. During the eruption, _____ ash flew into the air as lava flowed down the mountain.

12. This week Marcy learned a new _____ routine on the balance beam.

Part II: Pick two words from the box above. Use each in a sentence.

Example: ___Volcanic ashes settled all over the town.___

1. _____

_____

2. _____

_____

The Suffix *-ment*

The suffix *-ment* means "in a state of."

Examples: *amusement* means "in a state of amusing"

management means "in a state of managing"

ornament	encouragement	discouragement	punishment	argument
resentment	measurement	movement	~~amazement~~	merriment

Part I: Write the word from the box above that matches the meaning.

1. in a state of amazing   amazement

2. in a state of moving   _____

3. in a state of encouraging   _____

4. in a state of resenting   _____

5. in a state of arguing   _____

6. in a state of punishing   _____

7. in a state of being merry   _____

8. in a state of discouraging   _____

9. in a state of measuring   _____

10. in a state of being ornate (fancy)   _____

Part II: Some common words do not follow the rule for the meaning of the suffix *-ment*. Write each word's meaning. You may use a dictionary.

Example: environment   the conditions that influence the growth and development of living things

1. instrument _____

_____

2. basement _____

_____

3. department _____

_____

More Practice with the Suffix *-ment*

The suffix *-ment* means "in a state of."

movement	amazement	argument	ornament	experiment	discouragement
punishment	instrument	management	amusement	basement	encouragement

Part I: Choose from the box above the word that best completes each sentence and write it on the line. Each word is used once.

1. The worse the crime, the longer the _____ .

2. Jamie didn't like going down to the _____ because it was dark and scary.

3. That roller coaster is my favorite _____ park ride.

4. A shocked Jennifer stared in _____ at the flying rabbit.

5. His scientific _____ took three hours.

6. Ben made a Christmas _____ to hang on the tree.

7. They were yelling so loudly, we heard their _____ next door.

8. The coach gave her players lots of _____.

9. Great Deal's _____ just started a no-refunds policy.

10. The flute is the _____ my sister plays in the school band.

11. An earthquake is caused by a _____ of the Earth's plates.

12. When he lost the race, Cameron felt a deep sense of _____ .

Part II: Pick two words from the box above. Use each in a sentence.

Example: It rained so much that our **basement** flooded. _____

1. _____

    _____

2. _____

    _____

The Suffix -*ing* for Nouns

The suffix -*ing* can mean "the material used to." This suffix comes at the end of nouns (things).

When verbs end with the suffix -*ing*, it shows continuous action.

Examples: *icing* is the material used to ice a cake or cookie

plumbing is the material (pipes) used in a water or sewer system

Part I: Write the meaning of each noun.

Example: salad dressing ___material used to "dress" a salad___

1. carpeting _____

2. lighting _____

3. roofing _____

4. stuffing _____

5. clothing _____

6. bedding _____

7. tiling _____

8. leggings _____

9. siding _____

10. styling gel _____

11. flooring _____

12. frosting _____

Part II: Sort the 12 words above into one of three categories. Write the words in the correct place.

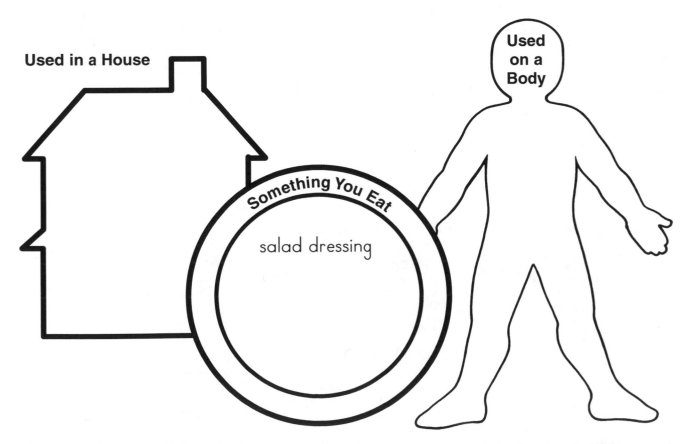

Used in a House

Used on a Body

Something You Eat

salad dressing

More Practice with the Suffix *-ing*

The suffix *-ing* can mean "the material used to." This suffix comes at the end of nouns (things).

When verbs end with the suffix *-ing*, it shows continuous action.

carpeting	icing	roofing	bedding	stuffing	lighting
dressing	plumbing	clothing	leggings	styling	tiling

Part I: Choose from the box above the word that best completes each sentence and write it on the line. Each word is used once.

1. Ashley used _____ gel to keep her hair in place.

2. The _____ around the shower had cracked and needed replacing.

3. Ahmed dug his bare toes into the thick, plush _____.

4. The old teddy bear was torn and had lost some of its _____.

5. We can find new sheets and pillowcases in the _____ department.

6. The child was dressed in layers and had _____ on beneath her pants.

7. A power failure caused the _____ to go out in the plane's cabin.

8. The little child stuck his finger in the cake's chocolate _____.

9. The building's _____ had problems, and one of the pipes burst.

10. Dana poured French _____ on her salad.

11. The builder ordered enough _____ shingles to finish the roof.

12. Since they are the same size, Madison and Lexie borrow each other's _____.

Part II: Pick two words from the box above. Use each in a sentence.

Example: ___The leprechaun wore green **leggings.**___

1. _____

_____

2. _____

_____

The Suffix *-ous*

The suffix *-ous* means "full of."

Words ending with the suffix *-ous* are adjectives (words that describe nouns).

    Examples: *courteous* means "full of courtesy"

               disastrous means "full of disaster"

Part I: For each definition, write an adjective ending with the suffix *-ous*.

Example: full of numbers*   numerous

1. full of marvel _____
2. full of continue* _____
3. full of danger _____
4. full of courage _____
5. full of miracle* _____

6. full of poison _____
7. full of humor _____
8. full of glamor _____
9. full of fame* _____
10. full of hazard _____

    * The base word spelling changes when you add the *-ous*.

A *synonym* is a word that means the same as another. *Dangerous* and *hazardous* are synonyms.

horrendous	enormous	joyous	dangerous	poisonous	courteous
numerous	~~gorgeous~~	humorous	marvelous	courageous	famous

Part II: Write the word from the box above that is the synonym of the word(s) given.

Word	Synonym	Word	Synonym
1. beautiful	gorgeous	7. wonderful	_____
2. well-known	_____	8. joyful	_____
3. many	_____	9. gigantic	_____
4. harmful	_____	10. brave	_____
5. polite	_____	11. awful; terrible	_____
6. toxic; deadly	_____	12. funny	_____

More Practice with the Suffix *-ous*

The suffix *-ous* means "full of."

continuous	courageous	courteous	disastrous	famous	numerous
humorous	enormous	marvelous	poisonous	horrendous	gorgeous

Part I: Choose from the box above the word that best completes each sentence and write it on the line. Each word is used once.

1. It looked like it would take days to clean up such an _____ mess.

2. The tiny flower girl looked _____ in her purple and white dress.

3. Two _____ firefighters bravely battled the blaze.

4. There were _____ people waiting in line.

5. The _____ snake coiled up and prepared to strike.

6. A _____ flow of people streamed through the gates of the amusement park.

7. Jake is _____; he always remembers to say "please" and "thank you."

8. The odor was so _____ that we started to gag.

9. The story was so _____ that we couldn't stop laughing.

10. We had a _____ time during our visit to New York City.

11. If this bridge washes out before the train gets here, it will be _____.

12. The _____ actress stopped to give us her autograph.

Part II: Pick two words from the box above. Use each in a sentence.

Example: ____I thought that joke was **humorous.**____

1. _____

_____

2. _____

_____

The Suffix *-al*

The suffix *-al* means "related to."

Example: *final* means "related to the end"

Part I: Add the suffix *-al* to the base word to form a new word.

Example: dispose* _____disposal_____

1. nature* _____
2. origin _____
3. refuse* _____
4. season _____
5. festive* _____

6. emotion _____
7. bury* _____
8. globe* _____
9. recreation _____
10. remove* _____

* The spelling of the base word changes when the suffix *-al* is added.

Part II: Write the meaning of each word.

Example: natural _____related to **nature**_____

1. personal _____
2. dismissal _____
3. accidental _____
4. rehearsal _____
5. approval _____
6. horizontal _____
7. professional _____
8. conditional _____
9. renewal _____
10. arrival _____
11. visual _____
12. continual _____

More Practice with the Suffix *-al*

The suffix *-al* means "related to."

natural	burial	disposal	emotional	festival	removal
global	original	pedal	refusal	seasonal	rehearsal

Part I: Choose from the box above the word that best completes each sentence and write it on the line. Each word is used once.

1. Mom threw the food scraps into the garbage _____.

2. When did you change your _____ plan for this new one?

3. Yesterday we ate tamales at the Mexican _____.

4. We took down the _____ display after Christmas was over.

5. The speaker became so _____ that he started to cry.

6. The _____ of a wart can be painful.

7. Our play was ready to present after only three weeks of _____.

8. These all- _____ foods do not contain any added colors or chemicals.

9. My class had a party to mark the _____ of our time capsule.

10. Your _____ to answer my questions is upsetting.

11. The post office offers _____ delivery of letters and packages.

12. In order to stop the car, the man stepped on the brake _____.

Part II: Pick two words from the box above. Use each in a sentence.

Example: ___Proper **disposal** of garbage means throwing it in a trash can.___

1. _____

_____

2. _____

_____

The Suffix *-ity*

The suffix *-ity* means "state of or quality of being."

> *Examples:* *equality* means "the state of being equal"
>
> *necessity* means "having the quality of being necessary"

Part I: Form new words by adding the suffix *-ity* to the base word.

Example: curious* _____curiosity_____

1. electric _____
2. disable* _____
3. generous* _____
4. author _____
5. necessary* _____
6. rare* _____

7. personal _____
8. captive* _____
9. similar _____
10. able* _____
11. humid _____
12. clear* _____

*The spelling of the base word changes when you add the suffix *-ity*.

Part II: Removing *-ity* from a word often changes it from a noun (thing) to an adjective (describing word). Write the adjective for each phrase given.

Noun Phrase	Adjective + Noun
1. Mom's generosity	_____generous_____ allowance (describes allowance)
2. women's equality	_____ treatment
3. high humidity	_____ day
4. basic necessity	_____ shelter
5. drill needs electricity	_____ drill
6. books' similarity	_____ books
7. animal's captivity	_____ animal
8. clarity of vision	_____ vision
9. Ethan's personality	_____ journal
10. child's curiosity	_____ child
11. Ryo's humility	_____ student
12. gown's simplicity	_____ gown

More Practice with the Suffix *-ity*

The suffix *-ity* means "state or quality of being."

necessity	ability	curiosity	electricity	rarity	humidity
similarity	personality	generosity	captivity	authority	identity

Part I: Choose from the box above the word that best completes each sentence and write it on the line. Each word is used once.

1. I see a lot of _____ between you and your brother.

2. A newborn baby does not have the _____ to walk or talk.

3. Water is a _____ for life.

4. Her cheerful _____ made people enjoy spending time with her.

5. Pets and zoo animals are kept in _____.

6. High _____ made us sweat as we hiked up the hill.

7. The _____ of the thief is still unknown.

8. A 2,000-year-old Egyptian vase in good condition is a real _____.

9. When the _____ fails, it's called a blackout.

10. Only the teacher has the _____ to change the password.

11. His _____ made Joshua enter the spooky, boarded-up building.

12. In a sudden burst of _____, Dad increased my allowance by $2 a week.

Part II: Pick two words from the box above. Use each in a sentence.

Example: ___The **similarity** between the two movies is surprising.___

1. _____

_____

2. _____

_____

The Suffixes *-er* and *-or*

The suffixes *-er* and *-or* mean "a person who."

Examples: a *driver* is a person who drives

an *advisor* is a person who advises (gives advice)

Part I: Change each word to show a person who performs the action.

Add *-er* to words 1–6:   swim   _____swimmer_____

Add *-or* to words 7–12:   operate   _____operator_____

1. teach _____

2. travel _____

3. sing _____

4. manage _____

5. speak _____

6. lead _____

7. sail _____

8. act _____

9. invent _____

10. dictate _____

11. supervise _____

12. instruct _____

Part II: Draw a line to match the person to their job.

1. realtor

2. dancer

3. doctor

4. instructor

5. tailor

6. barber

7. lawyer

8. firefighter

a. a person who changes clothes so they fit better

b. a person who practices law

c. a person who fights fires

d. a person who treats the sick

e. a person who sells real estate (houses, buildings)

f. a person who entertains others by dancing

g. a person who instructs (teaches)

h. a person who cuts hair

More Practice with the Suffixes -er and -or

The suffixes -er and -or mean "a person who."

actor	speaker	operator	teacher	swimmer	driver
traveler	singer	sailor	manager	doctor	leader

Part I: Choose from the box above the word that best completes each sentence and write it on the line. Each word is used once.

1. My _____ doesn't give homework on weekends.

2. The _____ honked her car horn at the pickup truck.

3. The _____ carefully set the broken bone.

4. The weary _____ had his flight delayed for six hours.

5. The telephone _____ gave me the phone number.

6. The store _____ had an idea to speed up the check-out lines.

7. The _____ completed nine laps in the pool.

8. A famous _____ opened the baseball game by singing the national anthem.

9. That _____ appeared in his first movie 10 years ago.

10. The team _____ was responsible for the project.

11. A _____ may go to sea for months at a time.

12. A guest _____ addressed our meeting.

Part II: Pick two words from the box above. Use each in a sentence.

Example: I want to be a famous **singer** when I grow up.

1. _____

_____

2. _____

_____

The Suffixes *-th* and *-port*

The suffix *-th* means "having the quality of."

The suffix *-port* means "to carry."

> *Examples:* hundredth means "having the quality of one hundred"
>
> export means "to carry goods out of a country"

Part I: Form words by adding the suffix *-th* to the base word. Write the word on the line.

Example: deep*   __depth__

1. steal _____   7. ten _____

2. strong* _____   8. warm _____

3. eight _____   9. long* _____

4. grow _____   10. heal _____

5. young* _____   11. dead* _____

6. true* _____   12. wide* _____

*The base word changes with the addition of the suffix *-port*.

Part II: Match the word to its meaning. Write the letter on the line next to the word.

_____ 1. import

_____ 2. airport

_____ 3. transport

_____ 4. seaport

_____ 5. passport

_____ 6. export

a. to carry from one place to another

b. a government booklet that lets you travel abroad

c. to carry things out of a country

d. a place where people and goods go to be carried by plane

e. to carry things into a country

f. a harbor where seagoing ships dock

More Practice with the Suffixes *-th* and *-port*

The suffix *-th* means "having the quality of." The suffix *-port* means "to carry."

warmth	seaport	length	strength	airport	export
passport	truth	transport	import	sixth	depth

Part I: Choose from the box above the word that best completes each sentence and write it on the line. Each word is used once.

1. Grocery stores in the U.S. _____ some bananas from Brazil.

2. You'll trip over your gown unless its _____ is shortened.

3. At the _____ we bought tickets for the next flight to San Francisco.

4. It takes _____ to lift weights.

5. How do you plan to _____ the elephant from Africa to the zoo?

6. After we came in from the cold, we enjoyed the _____ of the hot cocoa.

7. Farmers in Brazil _____ bananas to grocery stores in the U.S.

8. Tamara is the _____ of eight children.

9. The water's _____ was only 10 inches.

10. Without his _____, Randy couldn't enter Switzerland.

11. When the _____ finally came out, she was cleared of all the charges.

12. New York City is a busy _____ with lots of ships coming and going.

Part II: Pick two words—each with a different suffix—from the box above. Use each word in a sentence.

Example: I visited a **seaport** in Bar Harbor, Maine.

1. _____

   _____

2. _____

   _____

The Suffixes *-ry* and *-ery*

The suffixes *-ry* and *-ery* mean "occupation or place of business or product."

Examples: *surgery* is the occupation of a doctor who does operations

a *grocery* store is a place of business that sells groceries (food)

jewelry is an ornamental product a person wears (like a ring or bracelet)

Part I: Use a dictionary to write the definitions of the words below.

Example: nursery <u>a place where plants and trees are raised and sold</u>

1. refinery _____

2. cutlery _____

3. winery _____

4. forestry _____

surgery	jewelry	nursery	factory	grocery	refinery
bakery	pottery	forestry	winery	cutlery	dentistry

Part II: Sort the words in the box into three groups: places of business, products, and occupations. Write them on the correct box below.

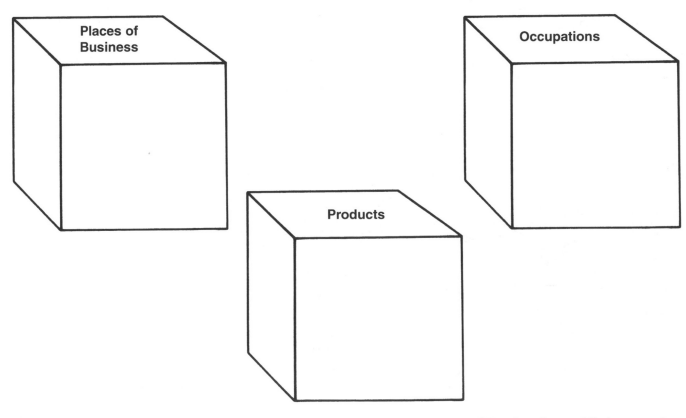

More Practice with the Suffixes *-ry* and *-ery*

The suffixes *-ry* and *-ery* mean "occupation or place of business or product."

surgery	forestry	chemistry	grocery	factory	bakery
nursery	pottery	jewelry	winery	dentistry	cutlery

Part I: Choose from the box above the word that best completes each sentence and write it on the line. Each word is used once.

1. A person working in _____ often has a job in a national or state park.

2. This _____ box has places for rings, necklaces, ear rings, and bracelets.

3. Joya went to the _____ store to buy the food for the party.

4. The wonderful smells coming from the _____ made us hungry.

5. The ancient _____ was chipped and cracked.

6. The school's _____ lab had chemicals, test tubes, and beakers.

7. We keep our _____ in this kitchen drawer.

8. He's always liked teeth, so he chose a career in _____.

9. We chose a Japanese maple tree from the _____.

10. The doctor soon learned to do eye _____.

11. This is the _____ where they make the tires.

12. During the tour of the _____, they tasted five different wines.

Part II: Pick two words from the box above. Use each in a sentence.

Example: _____ We bought some snacks at the **grocery** store. _____

1. _____

_____

2. _____

_____

Assessment 1

Directions: Darken the circle of the correct answer.

1. **The word *mislabeled* means**
   - (a) labeled wrong
   - (b) not labeled
   - (c) labeled again

2. **The word *overdone* means**
   - (a) done again
   - (b) done too much
   - (c) not done

3. **The word *co-workers* means people who**
   - (a) don't work
   - (b) work hard
   - (c) work together

4. **The word *self-respect* means**
   - (a) respect for oneself
   - (b) respect for others
   - (c) respect for animals

5. **The word *illiterate* means**
   - (a) not able to hear
   - (b) not able to speak
   - (c) not able to read and write

6. **The word *semisweet* means**
   - (a) too sweet
   - (b) half sweet
   - (c) not sweet

7. **The word *limitation* means**
   - (a) above the limit
   - (b) material used to limit
   - (c) having the quality of limiting

8. **The word *soloist* means**
   - (a) without a solo
   - (b) a person who does solos
   - (c) related to a solo

9. **The word *dramatic* means**
   - (a) do drama again
   - (b) related to drama
   - (c) a person who does drama

10. **The word *bedding* means**
    - (a) a tiny bed
    - (b) material used to make a bed
    - (c) too many beds

11. **The word *hazardous* means**
    - (a) half a hazard
    - (b) not a hazard
    - (c) full of hazard

12. **The word *counselor* means**
    - (a) counsel oneself
    - (b) a person who counsels
    - (c) not enough counsel

13. **The word *stealth* means**
    - (a) person who steals
    - (b) without stealing
    - (c) having the quality of stealing

14. **The word *refinery* means**
    - (a) state of refining
    - (b) person who refines
    - (c) place where things are refined

15. **The word *automatic* means**
    - (a) operating by itself
    - (b) related to an automobile
    - (c) part of an autograph

Assessment 2

Directions: Darken the circle of the correct answer.   Not all of the choices are actual words.

1. **Choose the word that means "wrong deed."**
    (a) undeed   (b) misdeed   (c) disdeed

2. **Choose the word that means "tax too much."**
    (a) overtax   (b) pretax   (c) retax

3. **Choose the word that means "host together."**
    (a) hostment   (b) hostess   (c) cohost

4. **Choose the word that means "many."**
    (a) century   (b) increase   (c) multitude

5. **Choose the word that means "not definite."**
    (a) indefinite   (b) definitely   (c) ildefinite

6. **Choose the word that means "100 years."**
    (a) century   (b) centennial   (c) centipede

7. **Choose the word that means "having the quality of reflecting."**
    (a) coreflect   (b) reflection   (c) reflectry

8. **Choose the word that means "having the quality of being precise."**
    (a) precisous   (b) precisor   (c) precision

9. **Choose the word that means "a person who practices terror."**
    (a) terrorist   (b) terrorism   (c) territory

10. **Choose the word that means "related to strategy."**
    (a) strategist   (b) strategic   (c) strategor

11. **Choose the word that means "the state of resenting."**
    (a) resentment   (b) resentous   (c) resenter

12. **Choose the word that means "material used to panel."**
    (a) flooring   (b) carpeting   (c) paneling

13. **Choose the word that means "full of miracle."**
    (a) miraclist   (b) miraclement   (c) miraculous

14. **Choose the word that means "the quality of being capable."**
    (a) capablision   (b) capability   (c) capablery

15. **Choose the word that means "related to culture."**
    (a) cultural   (b) self-culture   (c) culturist

Assessment 3

Directions: Darken the circle of the correct choice. All answer choices are actual words.

1. *autograph* is a synonym for
   - (a) pen
   - (b) graphics
   - (c) signature
   - (d) actress

2. *overdue* is a synonym for
   - (a) undone
   - (b) late
   - (c) tired
   - (d) early

3. *instructor* is a synonym for
   - (a) teacher
   - (b) sailor
   - (c) supervisor
   - (d) counselor

4. *humorous* is a synonym for
   - (a) ugly
   - (b) heavy
   - (c) happy
   - (d) funny

5. *assignment* is a synonym for
   - (a) passport
   - (b) textbook
   - (c) task
   - (d) announcement

6. *inability* is an antonym for
   - (a) unable
   - (b) disability
   - (c) responsibility
   - (d) ability

7. *import* is an antonym for
   - (a) export
   - (b) report
   - (c) transport
   - (d) seaport

8. *heroic* is an antonym for
   - (a) nasty
   - (b) cowardly
   - (c) tragic
   - (d) courageous

9. *multiple* is an antonym for
   - (a) decrease
   - (b) harmony
   - (c) single
   - (d) increase

10. *removal* is an antonym for
   - (a) lessen
   - (b) addition
   - (c) support
   - (d) subtraction

Directions: Darken the circle of the word that best completes the analogy. All answer choices are actual words.

Example: **rule** is to *wrong* as *law* is to _____illegal_____
   - (a) legal
   - (b) illegal
   - (c) make
   - (d) reject

1. *penny* is to *dollar* as *year* is to _____
   - (a) century
   - (b) anniversary
   - (c) centennial
   - (d) centipede

2. *fur* is to *soft* as *pudding* is to _____
   - (a) liquid
   - (b) chocolate
   - (c) hard
   - (d) semisolid

3. *baker* is to *bake* as *tourist* is to _____
   - (a) reply
   - (b) travel
   - (c) pay
   - (d) concentrate

4. *dark* is to *light* as *correct* is to _____
   - (a) sincerity
   - (b) coincidence
   - (c) mistaken
   - (d) inactive

5. *ring* is to *jewelry* as *blanket* is to _____
   - (a) plumbing
   - (b) bedroom
   - (c) closet
   - (d) bedding

Summary of Prefixes and Suffixes

Prefix	Means	Prefix	Means	Suffix	Means	Suffix	Means
mis-	wrong	*over-*	above; too much	*-tion*	state of; quality of	*-sion*	state of; quality of
co-	together	*multi-*	many	*-ist*	a person who does	*-ic*	related to
auto-	self	*self-*	self	*-ment*	in a state of	*-ing* (for nouns)	material used to
in-	not	*il-*	not	*-ous*	full of	*-al*	related to
cent-	one hundred	*semi-*	half	*-ity*	state or quality of being	*-er, -or*	a person who
				-th	having the quality of	*-ry, -ery*	occupation, product, or place of business
						-port	to carry

Answer Key

Page 4
Part I
1. misprint
2. misfit
3. misspoke
4. misjudge
5. misspell
6. misplaced
7. misfire
8. misleading
9. mismatch
10. misinformed
11. mistreat
12. misfortune

Part II
1. misunderstood
2. mismatched
3. misbehavior
4. misfortune
5. misspelled
6. mismanaged
7. mislabel
8. misquote
9. misprint
10. mistake
11. mislead
12. misjudge

Page 5
Part I
1. mistake
2. mismatched
3. mismanaged
4. misprinted
5. misleading
6. misplaced
7. misquoted
8. misfortune
9. misbehaved
10. misunderstanding
11. misshapen
12. misspelled

Page 6
Part I
1. overheard
2. overcooked
3. overgrown
4. overlooked
5. overeat
6. overboard
7. overdue
8. overseas
9. overlap
10. overweight
11. overtime
12. overslept

Part II
1. overweight
2. overlap
3. overlooked
4. overslept
5. overdue
6. overgrown

Page 7
Part I
1. overwhelmed
2. overflowed
3. overslept
4. overweight
5. overlap
6. overpass
7. overseas
8. overboard
9. overlooked
10. overgrown
11. overcooked
12. overdue

Page 8
Part I
1. f   6. g
2. e   7. d
3. h   8. i
4. j   9. a
5. b   10. c

Part II
put checks by the following words: co-star, coordinator, co-owner, copilot, co-author, coworker, co-host

Page 9
Part I
1. coincidence
2. coordinator
3. copilot
4. co-owners
5. co-payment
6. cooperate
7. co-author
8. cosign
9. co-hosts
10. coworker
11. co-exist
12. co-star

Page 10
Part I
1. multimedia
2. multilevel
3. multicolored
4. multitasking
5. multifamily
6. multipurpose
7. multimillionaire
8. multilingual

Answer Key *(cont.)*

Part II

1. d
2. g
3. i
4. l
5. k
6. a

7. b
8. c
9. j
10. f
11. e
12. h

Page 11

Part I

1. multipurpose
2. multicultural
3. multifamily
4. multicolored
5. multiplication
6. multiple
7. multilevel
8. multimillionaire
9. multilingual
10. multimedia
11. multitude
12. multitasking

Page 12

Part I

1. c
2. f
3. a
4. g

5. d
6. b
7. e

Part II

1. self-confident
2. self-help
3. self-interest
4. self-employed
5. self-destruct
6. self-centered
7. self-respect
8. self-defense
9. self-taught
10. self-pity

Page 13

Part I

1. self-confident
2. self-defense
3. automobile
4. self-destruct
5. autograph
6. self-taught
7. autopilot
8. self-pity
9. self-control
10. automatic
11. automated
12. self-employed

Page 14

Part I

1. not correct
2. not logical
3. not formal
4. not dependent
5. not visible
6. not legal
7. not sane
8. not accurate
9. not complete
10. not effective

Part II

1. insecure
2. inaction
3. illegal
4. inexpensive
5. illogical
6. infrequent
7. illegible
8. indirect
9. injustice
10. illiterate

Page 15

Part I

1. illegal
2. inaccurate
3. ineffective
4. informal
5. illogical
6. infrequently
7. incorrect
8. illegible
9. independent
10. invisible
11. incapable
12. illiterate

Page 16

1. semicircle
2. centennial
3. percent
4. centimeter
5. semester
6. semiretired
7. cents
8. century
9. semifinal
10. semiannual
11. centipede
12. semicolon

Page 17

Part I

1. century
2. semiretired
3. percent
4. cents
5. semisolid
6. semester
7. semicircle
8. centipede
9. semicolon
10. centennial
11. semifinals
12. centimeters

Page 18

Part I

1. attention
2. invention
3. pollution
4. direction
5. revolution
6. reflection
7. explanation
8. completion
9. determination
10. protection
11. reaction
12. quotation
13. repetition
14. prevention
15. combination
16. exclamation

Part II

drop final letter, add -tion:

attention
pollution
completion

drop final letter, add vowel + *-tion*:

determination
quotation
combination

change base word + -tion:

motion
revolution
explanation
repetition
exclamation

Page 19

Part I

1. repetition
2. quotation
3. motion
4. attention

5. caution
6. direction
7. pollution
8. suggestion
9. invention
10. location
11. options
12. reflection

Page 20

Part I

1. confession
2. inclusion
3. television
4. discussion
5. admission
6. comprehension
7. profession
8. extension
9. invasion
10. conclusion

Part II

1. decide
2. divide
3. exclude
4. conclude
5. explode
6. revise
7. invade
8. tense
9. confuse
10. permit

Page 21

Part I

1. conclusion
2. television
3. revision
4. division
5. confusion
6. professions
7. admission
8. permission
9. collision
10. discussion
11. explosion
12. decision

Page 22

Part I

(allow leeway in definitions)

1. person who practices art
2. person who practices bicycling
3. person who is in a colony

Answer Key (cont.)

4. person who plays piano
5. person who practices terror
6. person who does hair styling
7. person who practices biology
8. person who tours
9. person who does dental work
10. person who practices typing

Part II
1. specialist
2. scientist
3. soloist
4. pharmacist
5. journalist
6. chemist
7. pianist
8. typist
9. motorist
10. organist

Page 23
Part I
1. scientist
2. optimist
3. artist
4. tourist
5. cyclist
6. florist
7. journalist
8. pianist
9. colonist
10. chemist
11. dentist
12. pharmacist

Page 24
Part I
1. realistic
2. volcanic
3. romantic
4. angelic
5. dramatic
6. periodic
7. heroic
8. gymnastic
9. scientific
10. scenic
11. robotic
12. historic

Part II
1. related to electricity
2. related to allergies
3. related to robots
4. related to giants
5. related to horror
6. related to strategy
7. related to economy
8. related to tragedy
9. related to volcanos
10. related to metal

Page 25
Part I
1. gigantic
2. electric
3. allergic
4. tragic
5. medic
6. realistic
7. metallic
8. historic
9. comic
10. scenic
11. volcanic
12. gymnastic

Page 26
Part I
1. amazement
2. movement
3. encouragement
4. resentment
5. argument
6. punishment
7. merriment
8. discouragement
9. measurement
10. ornament

Part II
1. a device (as in one used to make music)
2. the part of a building below ground level
3. a part of a larger organization (company, government, school, etc.)

Page 27
Part I
1. punishment
2. basement
3. amusement
4. amazement
5. experiment
6. ornament

7. argument
8. encouragement
9. management
10. instrument
11. movement
12. discouragement

Page 28
Part I
1. material used to carpet a floor
2. material used to create light
3. material used to cover a roof
4. material used to stuff (a turkey, etc.)
5. material used to clothe a body
6. materials used to make a bed (pillows, sheets, blankets)
7. material used to tile walls or floors
8. material used to cover the legs
9. material used to side a house, barn, or building
10. material used to style hair
11. material used to cover a floor
12. material used to frost (a cake, etc.)

Part II
used in a house:
carpeting
lighting
roofing
bedding
tiling
flooring
siding
something you eat:
salad dressing
stuffing
frosting
used on a body:
clothing
styling gel
leggings

Page 29
Part I
1. styling
2. tiling
3. carpeting
4. stuffing
5. bedding
6. leggings
7. lighting
8. icing
9. plumbing
10. dressing
11. roofing
12. clothing

Page 30
Part I
1. marvelous
2. continuous
3. dangerous
4. courageous
5. miraculous
6. poisonous
7. humorous
8. glamorous
9. famous
10. hazardous

Part II
1. gorgeous
2. famous
3. numerous
4. dangerous
5. courteous
6. poisonous
7. marvelous
8. joyous
9. enormous
10. courageous
11. horrendous
12. humorous

Page 31
Part I
1. enormous
2. gorgeous
3. courageous
4. numerous
5. poisonous
6. continuous
7. courteous
8. horrendous
9. humorous
10. marvelous
11. disastrous
12. famous

Answer Key *(cont.)*

Page 32
Part I
1. natural
2. original
3. refusal
4. seasonal
5. festival
6. emotional
7. burial
8. global
9. recreational
10. removal
Part II
1. related to a person
2. related to dismissing
3. related to an accident
4. related to rehearsing
5. related to approving
6. related to the horizon
7. related to a profession
8. related to a condition
9. related to renewing
10. related to arriving
11. related to vision
12. related to continuing

Page 33
Part I
1. disposal
2. original
3. festival
4. seasonal
5. emotional
6. removal
7. rehearsal
8. natural
9. burial
10. refusal
11. global
12. pedal

Page 34
Part I
1. electricity
2. disability
3. generosity
4. authority
5. necessity
6. rarity
7. personality
8. captivity
9. similarity
10. ability
11. humidity
12. clarity

Part II
1. generous
2. equal
3. humid
4. necessary
5. electric
6. similar
7. captive
8. clear
9. personal
10. curious
11. humble
12. simple

Page 35
Part I
1. similarity
2. ability
3. necessity
4. personality
5. captivity
6. humidity
7. identity
8. rarity
9. electricity
10. authority
11. curiosity
12. generosity

Page 36
Part I
1. teacher
2. traveler
3. singer
4. manager
5. speaker
6. leader
7. sailor
8. actor
9. inventor
10. dictator
11. supervisor
12. instructor
Part II
1. e   5. a
2. f   6. h
3. d   7. b
4. g   8. c

Page 37
Part I
1. teacher   7. swimmer
2. driver   8. singer
3. doctor   9. actor
4. traveler   10. leader
5. operator   11. sailor
6. manager   12. speaker

Page 38
Part I
1. stealth
2. strength
3. eighth
4. growth
5. youth
6. truth
7. tenth
8. warmth
9. length
10. health
11. death
12. width
Part II
1. e   4. f
2. d   5. b
3. a   6. c

Page 39
Part I
1. import
2. length
3. airport
4. strength
5. transport
6. warmth
7. export
8. sixth
9. depth
10. passport
11. truth
12. seaport

Page 40
Part I
(Exact wording of definitions
will vary depending on the
dictionary used.)
1. a factory that refines
   (improves) metals, oil,
   sugar, etc.
2. utensils used to cut,
   serve, and eat food
   (silverware)
3. a place where wine is
   made
4. the profession of forest
   rangers who plant,
   manage, and care for
   forests
Part II
place of business:
factory
grocery
refinery
bakery

nursery
winery
product:
jewelry
pottery
cutlery
occupation:
surgery
forestry
dentistry

Page 41
Part I
1. forestry
2. jewely
3. grocery
4. bakery
5. pottery
6. chemistry
7. cutlery
8. dentistry
9. nursery
10. surgery
11. factory
12. winery

Page 42
1. a   9. b
2. b   10. b
3. c   11. c
4. a   12. b
5. c   13. c
6. b   14. c
7. c   15. a
8. b

Page 43
1. b   9. a
2. a   10. b
3. c   11. a
4. c   12. c
5. a   13. c
6. a   14. b
7. b   15. a
8. c

Page 44
1. c   1. a
2. b   2. d
3. a   3. b
4. d   4. c
5. c   5. d
6. d
7. a
8. b
9. c
10. b